Color Your World

Medallions 1

by Sue Doe Nym

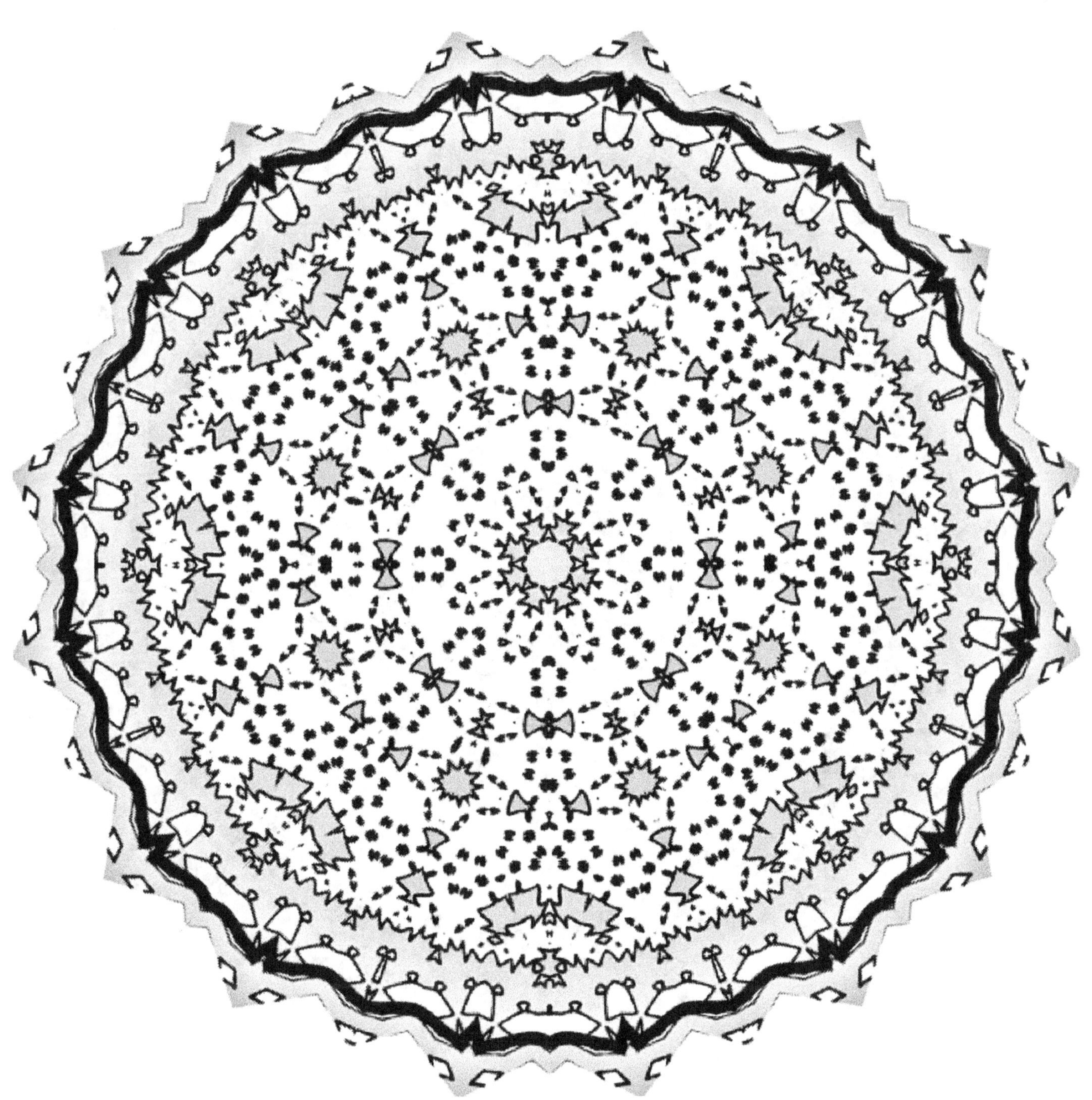

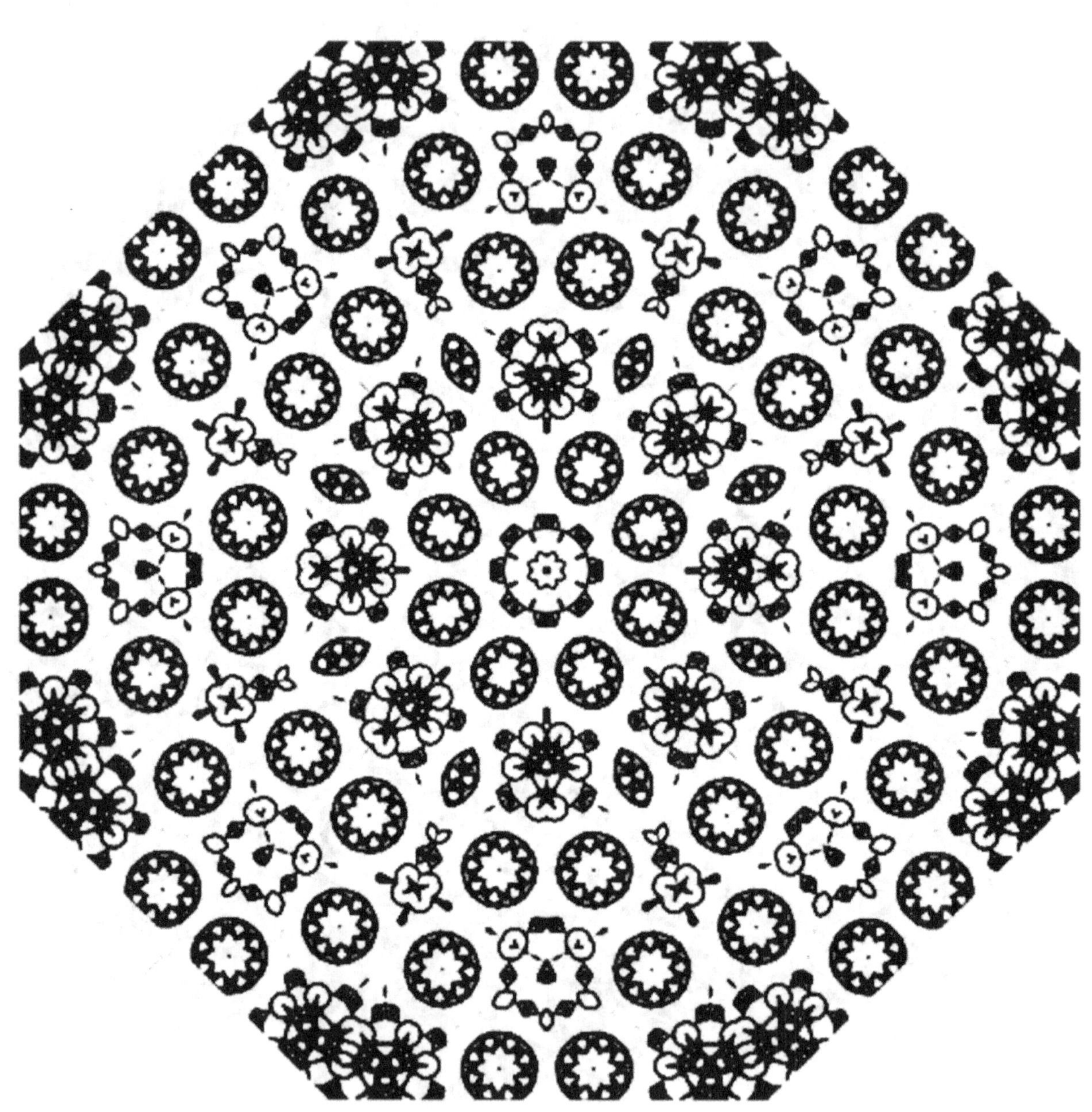

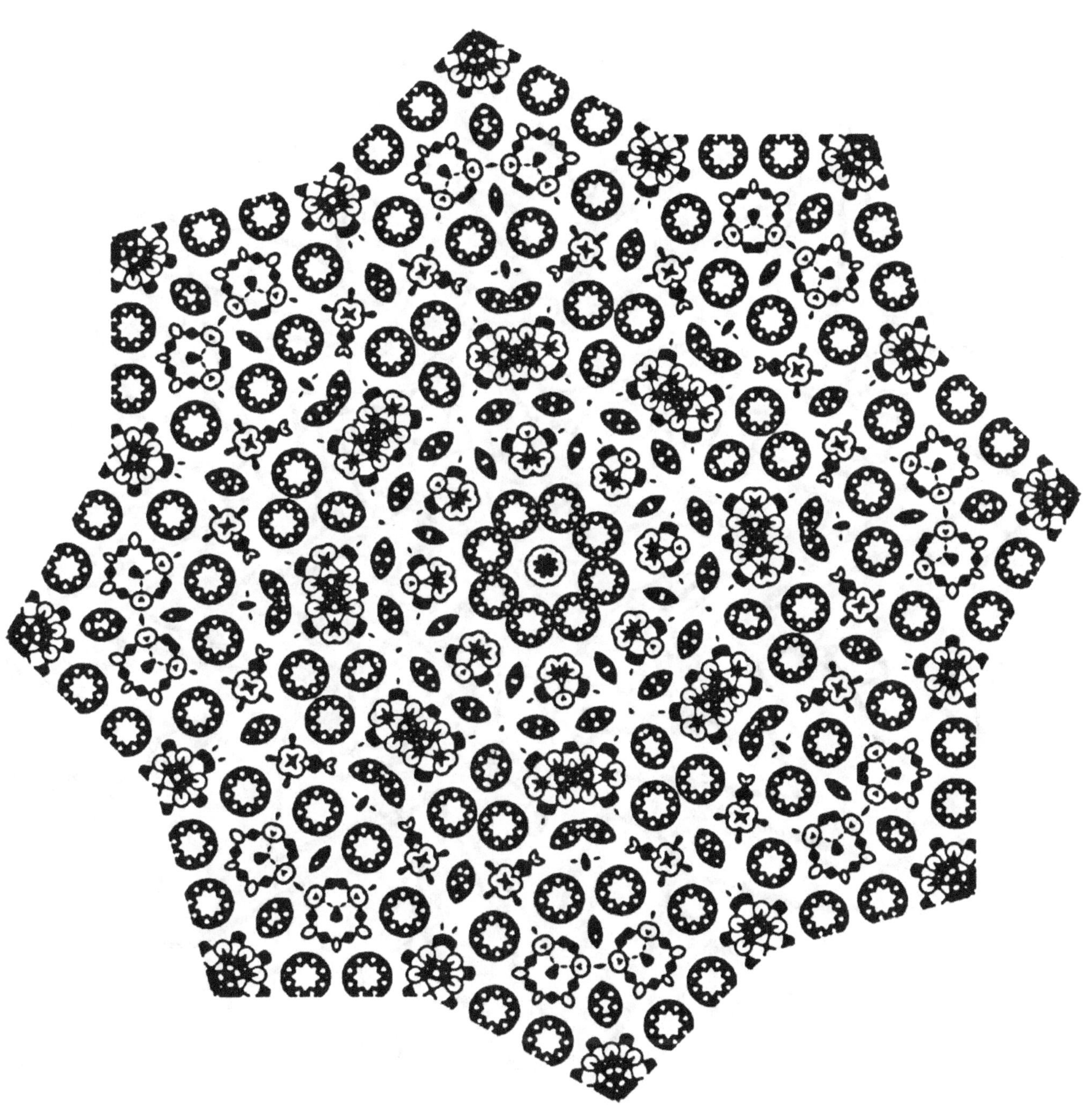

Want More From Sue Doe Nym Publishing

Puzzles:

Maze Craze Series
Sudoku - Fun For All Series
Sudoku Craze Series
Sudoku For The Holidays Series
Word Search
Cryptograms

Cookbooks:

Survival Guide - Venison And Game
Searchin' Recipes Series

Business:

Stop! The Truth Behind The Marketing Machine
Cross Your Legs This Is Gonna Hurt

Reading:

Making Magic - Mind Melts
A Moonbeam Tangle Revisited

Coloring Books:

Color Your World Series - Assorted